lululemon

Kaite Goldsworthy

Weigl

Published by Weigl Educational Publishers Limited
6325 10th Street SE
Calgary, Alberta T2H 2Z9
Website: www.weigl.ca

Library and Archives Canada Cataloguing in Publication

Goldsworthy, Kaite
     Lululemon / Kaite Goldsworthy.

(Canadian business)
Includes index.
ISBN 978-1-77071-213-3 (bound).--ISBN 978-1-77071-227-0 (pbk.)

     1. Lululemon Athletica--History--Juvenile literature.
I. Title. II. Series: Canadian business (Calgary, Alta.)

HD9948.5.C3L84 2012   j338.7'687   C2012-903545-9

Printed in the United States of America in North Mankato, Minnesota
1 2 3 4 5 6 7 8 9 0 16 15 14 13 12

092012
WEP250612

Senior Editor: Heather Kissock
Art Director: Terry Paulhus

Weigl acknowledges Alamy, CP Images, Dreamstime, Getty Images, iStockphoto, and Landov as the primary image suppliers for this title.

Every reasonable effort has been made to trace ownership and to obtain permission to reprint copyright material. The publishers would be pleased to have any errors or omissions brought to their attention so that they may be corrected in subsequent printings.

We acknowledge the financial support of the Government of Canada through the Canada Book Fund for our publishing activities.

Contents

1 ululemon athletica inc. is a Canadian company that designs and manufactures high-end, yoga-inspired athletic clothing. The company has achieved incredible success with its **technical fabrics** and functional designs. Its mission is "to create components for people to live long, healthy, and fun lives."

A Manifesto to Live By

To guide its employees and customers on this life path, the company has issued its corporate **manifesto**. Written on the company's shopping bags, the manifesto outlines philosophies and beliefs that the company feels are important to finding success in life. Some of its directives include "Do one thing a day that scares you" and "Listen, listen, listen, and then ask strategic questions." The manifesto

lululemon places its stores in locations that have a high number of people passing through. The company's stores can be found in shopping malls and on busy streets.

encourages people to live physically, intellectually, and emotionally engaged lives. It is this forward-thinking attitude that is projected in its products, programs, and customer service.

Redefining Casual Wear

lululemon is based in Vancouver, British Columbia. The company was founded in response to the growing number of women involved in athletics. It went on to create a **market** that did not exist before. lululemon began the trend toward yoga wear as everyday wear, influencing the way women dress and bringing yoga wear out of the studios and into streets, schools, and shopping malls.

lululemon manifesto

Stretching Out

Though still young, the company has gone from having a single location to more than 200 stores in six different countries. With its inspirational company manifesto and reputation for high quality, the **brand** continues to gain popularity as the company continues to expand.

lululemon athletica's unique and inventive approach to business, along with a well-designed product, have helped it to become an extremely successful Canadian, and now international, business. It continues to seek new opportunities to grow and share its philosophies toward living a long, healthy, and fun life.

Ω Many women wear lululemon clothing to make a fashion statement. They want to be seen as current and active.

Annual Sales

2011
Sales
$1,000.8
Million

- -

Distribution of Sales

United States
53%

43%
Canada

4%
International

- -

Employee Total as of 2011

 **5,807**

- -

Taking Stock

Founding Date
1998

Became Public
July 2007

Stock Symbol
tsx: LLL
nasdaq: LULU

The Founder: Dennis "Chip" Wilson

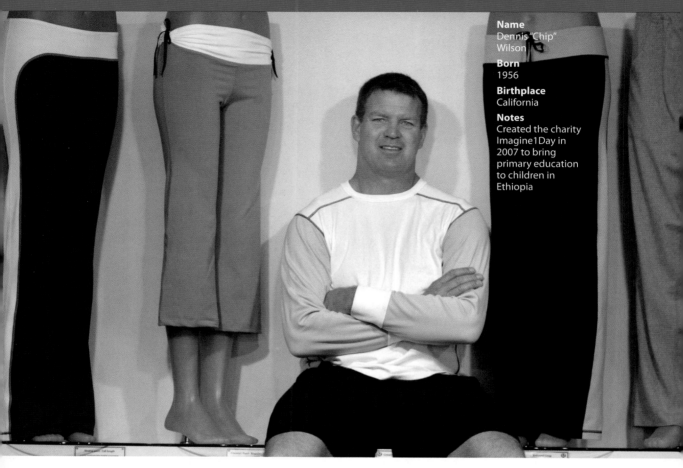

Name
Dennis "Chip" Wilson

Born
1956

Birthplace
California

Notes
Created the charity Imagine1Day in 2007 to bring primary education to children in Ethiopia

Chip Wilson has built a multimillion-dollar business out of his interest in yoga.

Dennis "Chip" Wilson founded lululemon athletica in 1998. Wilson was born in California in 1956, and moved to Calgary, Alberta, when he was five years old. Clothes and athletics were a big part of Wilson's life from an early age. His craft-oriented mother spent much of her spare time at a sewing machine making clothing and other creations. His father was a physical education teacher who had been named Athlete of the Year in high school.

Wilson's athletic prowess appeared early. His venue was water, where he became known as a strong swimmer. He even made Canada's national swim team in the 1970s. When his competitive swimming days came to an end, he turned to surfing and snowboarding. These sports helped him develop his first business.

Westbeach Surf

After graduating with a Bachelor of Arts in Economics from the University of Calgary, Wilson had to find a job. He went to California for the summer and came back with clothes that were not available in Calgary. He began making this style of clothing—mainly shorts—for his friends. Over time, this enterprise grew into a company Wilson called Westbeach Surf Ltd. The company would change its name to Westbeach Snowboard in the winter.

Inspired by Yoga

Wilson was the company's CEO until 1995, when he became head of design and production. He sold the company in 1997. During his time at Westbeach, Wilson learned much about the clothing business and how to make and market a product. He started lululemon athletica in 1998, after taking his first yoga class. This new company quickly began making a name for itself and its owner.

In 2004, Wilson was named Ernst & Young's Canadian **Entrepreneur** of the Year for Innovation and Marketing. In 2012, he made *Forbes Magazine's* "World's Billionaires" list, ranking ninth for Canada. In 2011, *Canadian Business Magazine* estimated his worth at $2.85 billion.

Wilson chose to step down as lululemon's chief innovation and branding officer in January 2012. He remains chairman of the company's **board of directors**, with a focus on helping the company grow. Wilson is married and the father of five boys. He lives in Vancouver, British Columbia.

The University of Calgary was founded in 1966. More than 30,000 students attend classes there every year.

Wilson continues to support the lululemon vision by living an active life.

"It would be impossible to not be in the athletic clothing business. That's all I think about." —Chip Wilson

Launching lululemon

In 1998, Chip Wilson took his first yoga class and was instantly hooked. He loved how healthy yoga made him feel and was soon attending classes regularly. Wilson noticed that many of the others in his class were not really dressed for yoga. At that time, much of the yoga wear available was made from fabrics that were not stretchy, lightweight, or breathable.

The original lululemon store, in Vancouver's Kitsilano neighbourhood, remains in operation and continues to serve the community.

Building on an Idea

Wilson had a passion for the technical side of athletic fabrics and clothing design. Having learned much while designing with Westbeach, he felt he could produce fabrics and clothing better suited to yoga. He believed yoga clothing should move

It's a
lululemon ⨀ **athletica**
First

FIRST STORE
lululemon's first store appeared on the corner of West 4th Avenue and Arbutus Street in Vancouver's Kitsilano area.

Kitsilano is located on the west side of Vancouver. The community has several shopping areas and is within walking distance to the ocean and downtown Vancouver.

Yoga by Night

The original design studio was part store, part yoga studio. During the day, Wilson would design and sell his clothing. In the evening, the space became a yoga studio. lululemon stores still operate this way. Staff in many stores often clear floorspace and move racks of clothing aside to hold free weekly yoga classes. Wilson originally envisioned having only one store, but he quickly realized how popular his clothing was. The first official retail store opened in the same Kitsilano neighbourhood in November 2000.

with the body and be lightweight. This would keep the wearer cool.

Wilson opened a design studio in the trendy Kitsilano neighbourhood of Vancouver and began to design and make his own yoga wear. He enlisted the help of local athletes and yoga instructors to test his clothing and critique his designs. The feedback he received helped him to create a new fabric called luon. He used this material to make his new clothing line. Word of this new clothing quickly spread through the yoga community. Soon, Wilson found his products in high demand.

Yoga requires participants to place their bodies in various positions. The clothing they wear must be flexible and comfortable.

FIRST U.S. STORE

In 2003, lululemon opened its first U.S. store in Santa Monica, California.

FIRST INTERNATIONAL STORE

lululemon entered the Australian market in 2004, opening a store in Melbourne, Victoria.

FIRST CHILDREN'S STORE

The company opened its first ivivva store in 2009. ivivva sells yoga wear for girls ages 6 to 12.

A Growing Company

The success of the first lululemon athletica led to the opening of stores in other parts of Canada. Customers flocked to the stores, attracted to the comfortable but durable clothing the company had developed. In 2003, lululemon athletica was recognized by the Retail Council of Canada as the Innovative Retailer of the Year in the "small store" category.

International Investors

By 2005, lululemon athletica had 33 stores operating across Canada and

ⓛ lululemon's early success helped the company lease prime retail space for its stores. In 2002, it opened a store on Robson Street, one of Vancouver's more upscale shopping areas.

was beginning its expansion into other countries. This expansion was aided by a deal with a U.S. company called Advent International, which bought a minority interest in lululemon athletica.

Advent International is a private **equity** firm. These types of companies **invest** in smaller companies and help them grow. Besides providing **capital**, private equity firms often act as business advisors to these small companies. The eventual goal of a private equity firm is to build the company to a point where it can be taken public or sold for a profit.

One of the first things Advent did to steer lululemon toward greater success was to begin organizing a senior management team. Chip Wilson vacated the position of chief executive officer (CEO) to become chairman and chief product designer. Robert Meers was hired to be the company's new CEO. Meers had previously worked with the Reebok athletic brand from 1984 to 1999, helping the company to grow and expand. Senior **executives** from several other well-known clothing companies, including Abercrombie & Fitch and J. Crew, were also added to the team. Together, these people took on the task of expanding the company's products and locations.

Within a year of this **restructuring**, the company had increased its sales by 50 percent in the United States. By 2007, it was ready to go public. lululemon had its **initial public offering** (IPO) in May of that year, with the company going public on the Toronto Stock Exchange (TSX) and NASDAQ two months later.

Reebok is one of the best-known names in athletic gear. The company was founded in 1895 as a shoe company. Today, it is owned by another athletic wear company, adidas.

NASDAQ is the second largest stock exchange in the world. It is located in New York City.

International Growth

Advent International's support allowed lululemon athletica to expand into other countries at a pace that would not have been possible otherwise. With an experienced senior management team and an increase in capital, lululemon secured locations in key markets in the United States and abroad.

U.S. Expansion

lululemon had opened its first store in the United States before Advent International bought into the company. The Santa Monica store had been operational since 2003. This location was selected because of its high number of yoga devotees.

Santa Monica is located in southern California. Its proximity to the beach provides residents with many opportunities to be active.

Advent helped lululemon identify other markets that would welcome its product. Stores soon opened in prime U.S. markets, including Boston, Los Angeles, Chicago, and New York. The timing of this expansion was critical. By 2005, the women's athletic wear industry was 25 percent larger than the men's. Yoga had increased in popularity as well, with 16.5 million yoga devotees in the United States alone at that time. lululemon both influenced and benefitted from the growing interest in yoga and women's athletic wear. By the time the company went public in 2007, there were almost 80 lululemon stores in the United States.

International Expansion

lululemon had also started expanding abroad prior to its association with Advent. With the help of New Harbour Yoga Pty Ltd., it had opened a store in Melbourne, Australia, in October 2004. Eight additional stores were opened over the next five years. In 2010, the company increased its interest in New Harbour Yoga Pty Ltd. to continue its expansion in the region. With more than 20 stores in Australia, lululemon expanded into New Zealand. Its first store there opened in 2011.

In October 2006, the company made a deal with Descente Ltd. to form lululemon Japan. With a store already opened in Tokyo, the partnership went on to open three more stores. In April 2008, lululemon closed operations in Japan in order to focus on the North American market.

New Markets

Expanding in the North American market meant expanding the company's customer base. In the fall of 2009, lululemon launched ivivva athletica, a line designed exclusively for girls aged 6 to 12, in response to its popularity with the younger age group. The first ivivva store opened in Vancouver, British Columbia. Expansion into Alberta and Nova Scotia soon followed. In recent years, lululemon has added clothing lines designed for running as well as a range of athletic clothing for men, bringing in a new segment of customers and further increasing **profits**.

Children's yoga classes are a growing trend. Many parents see yoga as a way for their children to develop self-esteem and body awareness in a non-competitive environment.

Locations

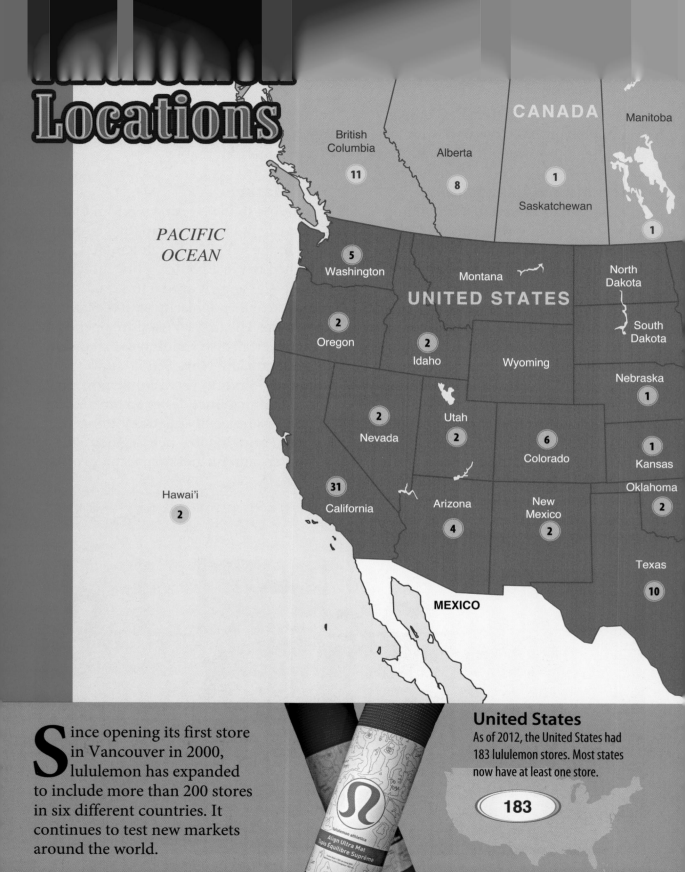

PACIFIC OCEAN

CANADA

British Columbia — 11

Alberta — 8

Saskatchewan — 1

Manitoba — 1

UNITED STATES

Washington — 5

Oregon — 2

Idaho — 2

Montana

Wyoming

North Dakota

South Dakota

Nebraska — 1

Nevada — 2

Utah — 2

Colorado — 6

Kansas — 1

Hawai'i — 2

California — 31

Arizona — 4

New Mexico — 2

Oklahoma — 2

Texas — 10

MEXICO

Since opening its first store in Vancouver in 2000, lululemon has expanded to include more than 200 stores in six different countries. It continues to test new markets around the world.

United States
As of 2012, the United States had 183 lululemon stores. Most states now have at least one store.

183

Prince Edward Island

Quebec

17

Ontario

4

Nova Scotia

1

Maine

1

ATLANTIC OCEAN

Vermont

2

New Hampshire

1

Massachusetts

6

Minnesota

3

New York

13

Rhode Island

1

Connecticut

3

Wisconsin

3

Michigan

3

Pennsylvania

6

New Jersey

6

Ohio

5

Delaware

4

Maryland

1

Iowa

Indiana

1

Washington D.C.

West Virginia

2

Illinois

9

Virginia

5

Kentucky

1

Missouri

2

North Carolina

4

Tennessee

4

South Carolina

2

Arkansas

1

Georgia

1

Alabama

5

Louisiana

Mississippi

3

Florida

12

Gulf of Mexico

THE BAHAMAS

PUERTO RICO

Canada

In 2012, Canada had at least 43 lululemon stores spread out across the country.

43

International

In 2012, Australia had the third largest number of lululemon stores, with 24 stores. Its neighbour, New Zealand, had three stores. Showrooms, or trial stores, were operating in other countries as well.

The lululemon Brand

ululemon has established itself as a recognizable brand in Canada, the United States, and Australia. The company is most popular with women aged 18 to 34. It has been able to brand itself as a supplier of premier yoga gear. Many consumers choose to wear the brand not just as athletic wear, but also to denote status. Shoppers consider lululemon clothing a luxury item because of its perceived quality and higher price point compared to other brands.

The Branding of Culture

The company's brand has developed into what is known as the lululemon culture. In keeping with the company's goal to help people "live longer, healthier, and more fun lives," this culture focusses not only on products but also on lifestyle.

In-store displays play a big role in promoting the lululemon brand. They show how the clothing and accessories come together to present an active, healthy lifestyle.

Increasingly health-conscious consumers want to invest time in themselves and their physical well-being. lululemon has been able to capitalize on this trend, convincing the consumer that spending money on a hoodie or a pair of yoga pants is an investment in health.

lululemon culture is also guided by the company manifesto. The manifesto promotes positive attitudes toward life. The statements in the manifesto serve to brand the company as one that promotes personal well-being. Many consumers are attracted to the company's inspirational approach.

Creating Relationships

The lululemon brand encourages a dialogue between the company and its customers. In fact, lululemon athletica uses customer testing and feedback in the design of its clothing. Staff and customers are invited to share their opinions on lululemon's clothing. Guests are encouraged to leave realtime feedback on chalkboards located by the change rooms in each store. The feedback is regularly sent to the company's customer support centre and used by the company to improve or create new products. By consulting directly with the people who use its products, the company can create the clothing its clientele wants and needs. This helps the company build relationships with its customers. As people become aware of their role in lululemon's product-development process, they stay loyal to the brand.

Team Yoga

The lululemon research and development team includes yoga and fitness instructors. These people test the company's products and advise lululemon on how the clothing fits, feels, and functions during use. Program participants may suggest changes or improvements to clothing. lululemon reviews these suggestions and alters its designs accordingly. This process takes more time, but lululemon believes it results in a better quality product and more support for the company's product lines.

What's in a Name?

lululemon is a fabricated name with no meaning. It came to Chip Wilson after an incident with the Japanese market when he was still running Westbeach.

Westbeach had added a skateboard brand to the company roster. Named homless, it sold mainly to the Japanese market. After a few years, Westbeach decided to stop making the homless products and focus on the surf and snowboard market for which it was known.

When the company's Japanese distributor realized that it was losing a popular product line, it asked Westbeach if it could buy the homless name. Westbeach agreed, but Wilson wondered why the name was so important. He eventually realized that the "L" sound is not found in the Japanese language. To the Japanese, the "L" sound was North American. Therefore, any product with that letter had to be authentically North American.

At that point, Wilson felt it was in his best interest to use the letter "L" in the name of his next company. He challenged himself to use at least three L's and began making up names. lululemon was one of his creations.

When it was time to name the new company, this name was put alongside 20 other names. Wilson showed the list to 100 people and asked them to pick their favourite. lululemon athletica won the vote.

The company's **logo** was chosen in the same survey. It was the logo for another tentative company name, athletically hip. The logo consists of a stylized "A."

The Art of Selling

lululemon promotes itself not only as a brand of clothing, but also as a set of beliefs and ideals. By involving the yoga community and its regular customers in its product development, the company creates valuable spokespeople for the company and its products. lululemon's approach to selling its brand has been highly effective.

The Power of Word of Mouth

Unlike many in the competitive clothing industry, lululemon has achieved success with very little traditional advertising. The company does not use television ads and only occasionally places print ads in yoga magazines. In fact, lululemon does not even have a traditional marketing department. Instead, it relies on word of mouth from customers.

Chandra Crawford is one of lululemon's elite ambassadors. Crawford is one of Canada's top female cross-country skiers. She won a gold medal at the 2006 Winter Olympics in Turin, Italy.

Word of mouth is one of the most powerful tools for promotion. Consumers are far more likely to believe the word of other happy, satisfied consumers who have nothing to gain by sharing their positive experience. The company benefits from this type of promotion in other ways as well. Word of mouth is free. The company does not have to invest much money in advertising.

Ambassadors

Every year, lululemon chooses "ambassadors" to test and review its clothing. Ambassadors are often local athletes or role models who represent the lululemon lifestyle and philosophy. They are listed on the company website by first name and by the city they represent. Large photos of each local ambassador hang in each store.

lululemon also has more than 60 elite ambassadors. These people are professional athletes who train or compete in lululemon clothing. Ambassadors are not paid, although all receive free clothing during their tenure. Having ambassadors wear the lululemon brand gains publicity and visibility for the company while assisting athletes in the community. This approach is considered **grassroots** advertising.

Media, Social Media, and the Internet

Like many companies in the age of social media, lululemon promotes its brand through pages on Facebook and Twitter, an official blog written by staff, and a series of instructional yoga videos on YouTube. lululemon has also gained media attention for its publicity stunts. For instance, at the opening of its Robson Street store in Vancouver, the company offered free lululemon clothing to the first 30 people who showed up naked.

lululemon has also created videos poking fun at the company and the yoga lifestyle and posted them on the internet. The videos are often so popular they go viral, becoming widely discussed and gaining more media coverage for the company.

lululemon manages the company's public profile with a brand-experience team. This group of employees ensures that the brand is properly represented in the media and online. It is also responsible for supporting store ambassadors.

lululemon sponsors Team Specialized-lululemon, a professional cycling team that competes in both road and track racing. By providing the team's clothing, lululemon ensures the visibility of its brand.

What's in Store?

lululemon offers yoga and fitness apparel for women and men. It also provides fitness accessories such as gym bags and yoga mats. All lululemon products are designed with features that are functional for the user.

Scuba Hoodie

The scuba hoodie is one of the most popular items sold by lululemon. This cotton fleece hoodie was inspired by the need for warm clothing after scuba diving in the cold waters of British Columbia. The deep hood, high collar, longer sleeve with thumbholes, and fitted wrists and waistbands make the hoodie even warmer. The "zipper garage," a flap of fabric that stops the zipper from scraping the chin, is a popular feature. The elastic zipper pull on women's clothing also doubles as an emergency hair tie

West Coast Hoodie

Similar to the scuba hoodie, the men's west coast hoodie features many of the same design elements, such as a deep hood and a "zipper garage." The hoodie has a unique offset zipper and a chest pocket for iPods.

Cool Racerback

Usually made from luon, this tank top is designed for activity. It is stretchable and breathable, allowing for comfortable movement. Seams are flat, so they do not rub or chafe the skin. The extra length helps ensure the top does not ride up. Racerback describes the style of the straps, which are in the centre of the back rather than over each shoulder. This allows the arms to move more freely.

Padded Run Sock

lululemon has begun producing clothing for runners as well as yoga enthusiasts. One of the company's newer products is the padded run sock for women. The socks feature extra padding in the heel and toe, known high-impact areas for runners. A reinforced area across the top of the sock protects the foot from blistering caused by laces. The socks are made from a moisture-**wicking** fabric called tactel. This helps keep the wearer's feet dry

Totebags

Totebags are a handy way to carry all of an active woman's athletic gear to class. lululemon offers a range of totebags for this purpose. Most bags have pockets and zippers to allow users to organize their possessions. Some bags even provide a separate compartment for storing clothing after the workout. Almost all bags have a strap or pocket for storing a yoga mat.

Groove Pant

The groove pant was one of the first products designed by lululemon. It remains the company's most popular yoga pant. Groove pants are made with the company's signature luon fabric. The flat seams and waistband make them a comfortable and popular choice for any activity. The pants also feature a hidden pocket tucked into the waistband for cards or keys.

Yoga Necessities

Yoga requires very little equipment, but lululemon provides their customers with the essentials. Yoga mats, mat holders, skidless towels, and water bottles are just some of the products the company offers to ensure a satisfying workout.

Running Gloves

For men who run year-round, lululemon has created the brisk run glove. Made with a material similar to luon, the gloves feature a mesh panel in the palm to allow for air flow. Wide cuffs allow the wearer to fit the gloves over the long sleeves of their running t-shirt. The finger space fits snugly so that the wearer can text or give someone a quick call without having to remove the gloves from their hands.

Heading up the Business

A company the size of lululemon requires the skills of many people. The corporate team is responsible for planning the company's future path. They decide where to put stores, how to market them, and how to keep running costs down. These are just a few of the executive positions at lululemon.

lululemon CEO: Christine Day
Education: Bachelor of Arts, Central Washington University, Executive Advanced Management Program, Harvard Business School
Joined lululemon: 2008

Chief Executive Officer

The chief executive officer (CEO) is usually the highest position in a company. A company's CEO is responsible for creating and executing the company's long-term goals. He or she is in charge of all aspects of the business. A CEO helps the company run smoothly, guiding it in a successful direction. CEOs oversee many departments and branches within the company, managing staff and delegating tasks. The CEO is present at company stock meetings and works with the Chief Financial Officer (CFO) on financial matters. The CEO usually reports to a board of directors. Generally, CEOs hold a high-level business or management degree.

Chief Financial Officer

A CFO is responsible for company finances. The CFO is sometimes known as the treasurer or finance director. He or she handles cash flow, balances the books, prepares detailed company financial reports, files quarterly and annual taxes and financial information on behalf of the company. The CFO may also be in charge of payroll. If the company is publicly owned, the CFO is responsible for reporting company financials to the **shareholders**.

lululemon Chief Financial Officer, Canada: John E. Currie
Education: Bachelor of Commerce, University of British Columbia
Joined lululemon: January 2007

lululemon Executive Vice President:
  Delaney Schweitzer
Education: Executive Advanced
  Management Program,
  Harvard Business School
Joined lululemon: 2002

Executive Vice President, Retail Operations North America

A vice president of retail operations is responsible for the day-to-day running of a company's stores. This executive sets sales goals for stores and plays an integral role in strategizing the steps needed to achieve those goals. Besides sales, the executive vice president of retail operations assesses the company's **bottom line** and develops ways to improve the profitability of the retail side of the business. He or she monitors store performance to determine possible market expansion and store closures.

Chief Information Officer

The chief information officer (CIO) of a company is responsible for all aspects of a company's **information technology** (IT) operations. This includes the management of all data centres, technical service centres, communication networks, computer program development, and computer systems operations. It is his or her job to find new ways to help customers and the organization profit from how data is used. He or she monitors the digital systems the company is using to ensure they are effective and user friendly. The CIO also monitors the security of all IT systems within the company.

lululemon Chief Information Officer:
  Kathryn Henry
Education: Egoscue University, National
  Academy of Sports Medicine
Joined lululemon: 2010

Working the Front Lines

At lululemon athletica, company success is very much a team effort. All employees work the retail floor, including the corporate office staff. The company feels this approach allows customer feedback to reach **head office** directly.

Strategic Sales

lululemon's strategic sales team works directly with yoga studios, fitness centres, and spas. Team members introduce these businesses to the company's products and culture. Their goal is to find new places to market and sell lululemon's products. The strategic sales team looks for companies that share similar goals and outlooks with lululemon. Through effective communication and education, the team

lululemon's strategic sales team knows that the company's clothing is functional in a variety of fitness settings. The team expands the reach of the brand by selling lululemon products in related markets, such as fitness centres and pilates studios.

builds relationships with these companies and helps them see the benefits of stocking lululemon's athletic gear.

Store Managers

lululemon's store managers are in charge of the daily operations of their individual stores. This includes supervising staff, serving customers, meeting sales targets, and **merchandising** the company's products to encourage sales. Managers are also responsible for presenting the corporate brand and culture to store employees and customers. Most store managers have a solid background in retail sales and service.

Educators

At lululemon, retail store employees are called educators. This is how the company defines the role they take on with each "guest," or customer. An educator directly affects whether guests feel welcome, make purchases, and return for more. Each location hires multiple educators. Educators work with store guests, educating them about both the clothing and the lululemon culture. Educators must have working knowledge of all the products lululemon sells. They help guests select appropriate clothing and accessories

Educators play a key role in encouraging return customers. They must be able to open and maintain a positive dialogue with people visiting the store.

and assist them with finding sizes. Educators are responsible for effectively managing their time with each guest based on the customers' needs.

Store managers and in-store staff wear lululemon clothing at work to promote the company's products and lifestyle.

FAQs

1 lululemon operates on a variety of levels, from corporate to front line. Anyone wanting to become a member of the team should learn more about the company and its operations.

WHERE DOES LULULEMON MANUFACTURE ITS CLOTHING?

lululemon is a global manufacturer, partnering with factories in 15 different countries, including Canada and the U.S. Some factories produce the fabric exclusive to lululemon, while others cut and sew the garments. lululemon searches for manufacturing partners who are responsible and ethical. Factories must provide a safe, clean, and healthy working environment for their workers.

WHAT IS A CODE OF CONDUCT, AND DOES LULULEMON HAVE ONE?

A code of conduct is a set of rules or standards that the company has promised to work by. lululemon's code of conduct includes refusing to use children or forced labour in factories and ensuring that all employees receive fair wages and benefits. The company has also committed to a safe work environment free of harassment and discrimination.

WHERE IS LULULEMON'S HEAD OFFICE?

lululemon's head office is located on Cornwall Avenue in Vancouver, British Columbia. The company's guest education centre is located in nearby Burnaby. The company's customer service representatives work from this location.

DO OTHER STORES SELL LULULEMON CLOTHING?

Only the lululemon athletica stores and website sell the company's full line of clothing. Certain yoga, Pilates, and fitness studios may be strategic sales partners. This means they can sell a limited selection of clothing. Studios must apply to the company and be approved to do this.

HOW IS LULULEMON LISTED ON THE STOCK MARKET?

lululemon is a publicly traded company on both the Toronto Stock Exchange and NASDAQ. On the TSX, it is listed under the LLL symbol. On NASDAQ, it is listed under the LULU symbol.

WHY DOES LULULEMON MAKE ITS OWN FABRIC?

lululemon is vertical retailer. This means it makes and designs not only clothing and accessories, but also the innovative fabrics used to make the garments. The company creates, and therefore controls, every aspect of its products. This allows lululemon to produce the high quality fabrics and clothing for which they have become known.

The Guest Experience

lululemon works hard to give its customers quality products and quality service. The company is constantly experimenting with new fabrics and clothing ideas. Staff training programs coach employees on how to convey lululemon culture and products to customers so that they feel inspired to live a healthy life. Building relationships with customers that go beyond a sales focus helps give lululemon an edge in the marketplace. The company has taken several steps to differentiate itself from its competitors.

Along with its in-store events, lululemon often holds yoga classes outdoors in local parks to help promote both the store and the lululemon lifestyle.

The lululemon Boutique

lululemon stores are designed to have an exclusive **boutique** feel to them. Like a number of other successful companies, such as Apple, lululemon stores operate on a salon-style business model. This means that store staff go beyond selling products. They engage in a dialogue with the customer, whether sharing ideas or discussing technology. In the case of lululemon, staff share the idea of living a healthy, positive lifestyle. Besides offering free in-store yoga classes, staff may also help a guest reach a fitness goal by offering one of the company's goal-setting worksheets.

lululemon was one of the first clothing stores to use this model. In fact, it was the original concept behind Chip Wilson's first lululemon store. It is an increasingly popular trend in retail sales.

Welcome to the Store

When guests arrive at a lululemon store, they are greeted by an educator as soon as they walk through the door. This shows the guests that lululemon is interested in them and wants to help. Educators are trained to know the products they sell and work with the guest to select the right ones. The goal of stores and educators is to identify with their customers and make them feel part of the lululemon community.

Inspiring Thoughts

Throughout the store, slogans and uplifting messages such as "Do it now!" are posted. These notes promote proactive living and inspire positive thinking. They often echo the statements found in the company manifesto. Selling the ideas of self improvement, positive thinking, and goal setting along with exercise and lifestyle clothing allow lululemon athletica to connect with its customers.

Ω Unlike most chain stores, lululemon shops are designed to project a local, homespun feel. This image extends from the store appearance to the friendly staff.

Ω Inspiring words and sayings can be found sprinkled throughout a lululemon store. They often greet people before they even enter the store.

Giving Back

The following text appears on the chalkboard calendar in the image:

5   10-11A zumba w/6ita
6   10-11A yoga IN bryant park
7
8   6-7P yoga IN bryant park
9   together we stand. 3PM: yoga w/Matt @ jiva 7PM: film screening @ jiva
10   9AM: yoga w/matt 11AM: yoga w/matt@
12   10-11A yoga w/jessica
13   10-11A yoga IN bryant park
14
15   caponyasa
16   6-7P yoga IN bryant park
17   9-10A yoga w/joelle
19   10-11A SNAP POP + ROCK w/snapshot & Wandee Pop
20   10-11A yoga IN bryant park
21
22   6-7P yoga IN bryant park
23
24   9-10A yoga w/lilia
26   10-11A boogie box w/katie
27   10-11A yoga IN
28
29   caponyasa 6-7P yoga IN park @ PURE WEST
30   9-10A

BREATHE DEEPLY

lululemon athletica believes strongly in community involvement. This goes beyond the local community, extending into corporate responsibility on a global level. The company developed its corporate social responsibility (CSR) department to create community legacies through grassroots actions and company actions.

Grassroots Actions

The company sees grassroots actions as those it inspires in its employees and customers. By promoting healthy living and environmental responsibility as part of its culture, the company expects that people involved with the company will in turn make positive changes in their own communities. Each store has a coordinator to organize local events as well as a community bulletin board where community actions and events are posted.

The in-store event board helps maintain the feeling of community lululemon promotes. It serves as an open invitation to customers and other store visitors to participate in lululemon culture.

Besides its yoga classes, lululemon stores provide the public with in-store seminars and activities that reflect lululemon culture. Seminar topics can range from goal-setting to the needs of local non-profit organizations in the community. Some stores have even organized informal running groups for their customers. On certain days, both customers and store staff get together for a scenic run through their community.

Company Actions

lululemon also creates legacies as a company. Company actions are those that happen within the company itself and work to improve the community. They include partnering with responsible, ethical manufacturers and making a commitment to produce less waste.

Environmental Stewardship

"What we do to the earth, we do to ourselves" is an idea expressed in the lululemon manifesto. In 2005, lululemon established a program to keep track of its impact on the environment. The goal was to find ways to reduce the company's **environmental footprint**.

lululemon worked with a team of environmental specialists to help determine ways to become more eco-friendly and energy efficient. As a result, the company has reduced waste in its factories, support centres, and stores, saving both money and the environment. Stores recycle and offer reusable bags. Shipping is done in reusable containers. New stores are designed and built using green practices. Stores are located near transit so they are easily accessible. Staff are encouraged to bike or car pool to work when possible.

Charitable Giving

lululemon builds relationships with customers through its charitable activities. A charitable donation program in each store allows customers to select charities for lululemon to support. Events such as the Flip Flop Soiree, which supports Vancouver's Centre for Integrated Healing, give lululemon the chance to give back to the communities that support them.

City transit helps reduce the pollution a city generates as it moves more people at one time than a car can.

lululemon packages customer clothing in reusable shopping bags that are made from a plastic called polyproylene. The material is 100 percent recyclable.

Competitors

The popularity of yoga wear has increased dramatically with the success of lululemon. As a result, many clothing companies have launched their own lines of yoga and fitness wear. lululemon currently has three main competitors—adidas, Nike, and Under Armour.

adidas

adidas is the largest sportswear manufacturer in Europe and second largest in the world. adidas products are sold in more than 170 countries. Unlike lululemon, adidas manufactures goods for many different sports. The company aims to offer choice while keeping the adidas brand current and distinctive. Most adidas products are recognized by their three-stripe and clover leaf logos. The company has a large following of loyal repeat customers. adidas has successfully used both advertising and sponsorship to build the brand's reputation. The company sponsors worldwide organizations, teams, and events, including the National Basketball Association (NBA), numerous international rugby and soccer teams, and even the 2008 Olympics in Beijing.

While lululemon's **demographic** is largely female, adidas is popular with both men and women. Comparable yoga wear products offered by adidas tend to be less expensive than those of lululemon. adidas aims to be a brand for everyone, from professional athletes to schoolchildren, rather than having the more defined and exclusive target market that lululemon has. Like lululemon, adidas is focussed on providing good value and high quality, maintaining the brand loyalty it has built.

Nike

Since 1972, U.S. company Nike has been designing and selling athletic wear for men, women, and children. Nike is the largest manufacturer of sportswear in the world and is the owner of several other

well-known brands, including Converse, Hurley, and Umbro. Like adidas, Nike makes products for numerous sports. Its products are available in more than 160 countries.

The Nike brand is instantly recognizable by the company's "swoosh" logo. Like adidas, Nike has very strong brand loyalty and an excellent reputation for quality. Nike has won awards for its creative advertising campaigns, which have featured well-known athletes and catch phrases such as "Just Do It." Nike's product pricing is slightly higher than adidas and similar to lululemon.

Under Armour

Founded in 1996, Under Armour is a U.S. company whose mission is to "make all athletes better through passion, design, and the relentless pursuit of innovation." Under Armour manufactures sportswear for men, women, and children for a variety of different sports. Its products are available in 27 countries. The company has successfully cornered the market on performance moisture-wicking undergarments and continues to expand into other types of products. Smaller than Nike and adidas, Under Armour is similar to lululemon in size and specialty market.

Under Armour uses both advertising and sponsorship to promote its brand. The company is the official supplier to a number of professional sporting associations, including the National Football League (NFL) and the Toronto Maple Leafs. Like lululemon, Under Armour is gradually gaining international recognition. However, it is not yet at the same level as Nike and adidas. Under Armour prices are generally lower than lululemon for comparable items of clothing. Under Armour's demographic is largely male, although the company is gaining popularity with women.

Charting Success

lululemon's Demographic Appeal

lululemon targets its products to 32-year-old women. However, the company's products appeal to a broad age range, and customers can be anywhere from 15 to 65 years old.

32 year olds

15 year olds

65 year olds

Chain Growth

The success of lululemon is apparent in its store development.
Over a six-year period, the company more than tripled its store count.

37 STORES — **2005**

51 STORES — **2006**

81 STORES — **2007**

113 STORES — **2008**

124 STORES — **2009**

138 STORES — **2010**

Market Size (CAN $ in Billions)

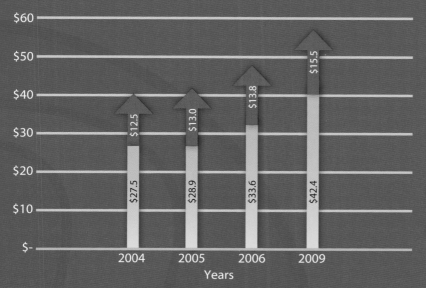

	2004	2005	2006	2009
Core Athletic	$12.5	$13.0	$13.8	$15.5
Activewear/Everyday	$27.5	$28.9	$33.6	$42.4

Years

Sales of active and athletic wear have seen steady growth in recent years, with sales exceeding $50 billion by 2009.

Activewear/Everyday

Core Athletic

Sales
(CAN $ in Millions)

Year		Amount
2009	$$$$$$$$	452.9
2008	$$$$$$$$	353.5
2007	$$$$$$	269.0
2006	$$$$$	148.0
2005	$$	84.1

Increased stores and a growing reputation have helped lululemon increase its sales every year.

Division of Sales

82%
Retail Stores

8%
Direct Sales
(Online)

11%
Other
(Wholesale, showrooms, warehouse sales)

The majority of lululemon's sales come from its retail stores. The company has, however, begun to focus on the online market. As this happens, the percentage of direct sales will increase.

Innovation and Technology

1 lululemon is a successful company because of its ability to think creatively. This innovative spirit was apparent in the company's beginnings, when Chip Wilson decided to make a fabric that would provide the stretch and durability that athletic activities require. Since the development of luon, the company has

FABRIC

Luon

Luon is a pre-shrunk, breathable, stretchable fabric made from nylon and Lycra. Unlike cotton, Luon wicks moisture away from the body, keeping the wearer dry and comfortable. It also retains its shape better than other fabrics. Luon is used in most of lululemon's yoga wear and is exclusive to the company.

SUSTAINABILITY

Oqoqo

In 2005, lululemon introduced a new clothing line called Oqoqo. Designed to tap into the movement toward **sustainable** living, the clothing was made from 75 percent natural, **organic** materials, such as bamboo, hemp, and soy. The company set up Oqoqo stores in Vancouver and Victoria, British Columbia. However, the line was later merged with the regular lululemon products.

FABRIC

Silverescent

Silverescent is an anti-bacterial fabric designed by lululemon to reduce the odour caused by sweat. Silver is known to inhibit the growth of odour-causing bacteria. When it is bonded to the threads in a garment, the bacteria attach themselves to the silver, and the odour is contained. Silverescent luon retains its shape while controlling body odour.

continued to search for new ways to make athletic wear.

The company has also been innovative in the way it sells its products. lululemon is constantly evolving in order to meet the needs of its market and to increase its customer base.

FABRIC

Vitasea

Vitasea is a fabric made from cotton, spandex, and SeaCell, a yarn made from seaweed. The addition of the SeaCell yarn makes a fabric that is softer than normal cotton. Like luon, Vitasea is pre-shrunk. It retains its shape and softness after washing. lululemon uses vitasea mainly in its t-shirts.

TEST MARKETS

Showrooms

When lululemon wants to test a new market, it starts by opening a showroom in the area. The showroom is a temporary store. For a limited time, the local community will be able to experience the lululemon culture and purchase the company's products. Events, parties, and educational sessions with local health and fitness experts are held to see how effective a lululemon store would be in this community.

ONLINE SALES

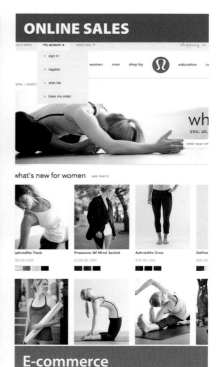

E-commerce

In April 2009, lululemon athletica expanded into **e-commerce**, selling online. Direct selling to customers through the company's website has a low **overhead** cost. No store is needed. A warehouse facility and staff are all that is required. Every year, the percentage of lululemon's annual sales made directly to the customer increases. The company currently ships to more than 53 countries worldwide.

Facing the Challenge

E very company has the occasional misstep. This is most common when a small company begins to expand. One of lululemon's most significant missteps occurred when the company began its expansion into the United States. The timing, the selected markets, and the pace of the expansion all contributed to challenging times for the company.

Rapid Expansion

After lululemon athletica opened its first U.S. store in 2003, the company was eager to continue expanding. In 2008, the company quickly opened 35 stores throughout the country. The U.S. stores rapidly became the least productive stores in the history of lululemon. At the time, the United States was in the middle of a financial crisis. Consumers, affected by a **recession**, were careful with their money

Companies are always reliant on a strong economy. People do not shop as often or for as much when the economy is sluggish.

and less likely to spend. lululemon had too many stores and not enough customers. The stores were not performing well enough to compensate for the money that lululemon had spent on their development.

The Learning Curve

Facing such a challenge ultimately had a positive effect on the company. The experience offered lululemon's executive team the chance to examine the strategies it had used for the expansion and make some needed changes. The team realized that it had rushed into the expansion without enough research. It concluded that the team should have analyzed the

 Christine Day and other lululemon executives regularly attend retail summits and conferences to discuss and track industry trends. This helps the team assess future plans for the company

A New Approach

As a result of this experience, the company now conducts thorough research before opening stores in a new city or location. It assesses locations in terms of demographics, **traffic** levels, and compatibility with lululemon culture. New stores are opened in cities and neighbourhoods that will be able to support the range of products that lululemon offers. The company also has a planned order of expansion, choosing to open in some locations or cities before others. The change in strategy has paid off for lululemon. Locations that have opened under this plan of action have been far more profitable than the stores that opened during the 2008 expansion. However, lululemon, like all companies, is still vulnerable to troubled economic times and remains watchful of market fluctuations.

communities the company was moving into and the demographics of the people living there. The executive team knew that future success would depend on the company becoming fully educated before expanding into new markets. It would also require a slower approach to expansion.

 Location is one of the most important factors when planning a store. To have a solid chance at success, it must be in a high-traffic area and close to the clientele it wants to serve.

The Future

Competition in the athletic wear market has increased dramatically since lululemon athletica began. Both financial experts and the company forecast further success for lululemon in the future. lululemon is preparing for this future through strategic planning that will see it grow its customer base, set up more stores, and take steps to reduce running costs.

Strategic Growth Opportunities

More lululemon stores and showrooms are being introduced into the U.S. market all the time. The company has an ultimate goal of 300 stores throughout the United States. lululemon plans to continue its

Hong Kong has a population of more than 7 million. With such a high number of potential customers, it will be a lucrative market for the lululemon brand.

expansion in the international market with the launch of stores in Hong Kong and the United Kingdom in the next few years. Showrooms were set up in both London and Hong Kong to help determine the potential of the market. The use of showrooms to test markets before moving to a full store has worked well for the company in the past. It plans to continue showrooms as a location-scouting strategy.

Encouraging Sales Growth

Many of the stores lululemon opened

in recent years had first-year sales that would normally not be seen until the third year of business. The company plans to continue this strong sales trend by adding new designs and expanding product lines. The company has already moved into running wear and men's wear. It has also developed a swimsuit line. Building a mixed and wide-ranging inventory brought lululemon much success in 2011, causing the company to raise its net **revenue** estimate by $30 million in January 2012. lululemon plans to continue to broaden its inventory into the future. Store educators and their connection with guests also continue to be a key part of the sales strategy for lululemon.

Growth of E-commerce Division

Introduced in 2009, lululemon's e-commerce division accounted for eight percent of the company's sales in 2010. lululemon aims to continue this growth by improving its information technology systems and company website. The company has also launched a website for lululemon Australia, and plans to do the same for both the Hong Kong and United Kingdom stores.

Building relationships with customers is key to lululemon's success as it promotes customer loyalty. A sense of belonging encourages customers to return to the store to make purchases.

1998 Chip Wilson founds lululemon.

2000 Chip Wilson develops a new material called luon.

2000 The first lululemon store opens in the Kitsilano area of Vancouver.

2002 The second Vancouver location opens on Robson Street.

2003 The first U.S. location opens in Santa Monica, California.

2005 The Oqoqo brand and stores are launched.

2005 On December 8, lululemon announces that the private equity firm Advent International has bought a minority interest in the company. Robert Meers is appointed CEO.

2006 On October 2, lululemon partners with Descente Ltd. to form lululemon Japan Inc.

2006 By October, the company has 40 stores in North America and one in Australia.

2007 In May, lululemon announces a Limited Public Offer (LPO).

2007 On July 27, lululemon goes public on the Toronto Stock Exchange (TSX) and NASDAQ.

2008 lululemon opens 35 new stores in the United States.

2008 In April, the company announces that it is closing the four stores opened in Japan.

2008 On April 2, Christine Day becomes president of lululemon after Robert Meers retires.

2009 On April 15, lululemon launches its e-commerce site.

2009 lululemon announces the creation of the ivivva athletica stores for girls aged 6 to 12. The Oqoqo brand is blended in with lululemon.

2010 lululemon announces it has increased it equity interest in its Australian partner New Harbour Yoga Pty Ltd.

2011 lululemon announces the official location of the company Global Store Support Centre in Kitsilano, where the company began.

2011 By May, lululemon has 142 stores in North America and Australia.

2011 In August, ivivva launches its Canadian online store.

2011 By October, lululemon has 165 stores throughout North America and Australia.

2012 Chip Wilson steps down as chief innovation and branding officer, but stays on as chairman of the board of directors.

Top 10

Every summer since 2006, lululemon has offered free **"guerrilla yoga"** classes on Parliament Hill. These classes are held with little notice, but have been known to attract more than 500 people at one time.

All **lululemon** stores offer **complimentary hemming of pants purchased there.**

Eleven lululemon stores have floors made from **reclaimed wood and building materials.**

lululemon provides showers for employees at some store locations so that they can reduce their **environmental footprint** by walking, running, or biking to work.

Christine Day was named **CHIEF EXECUTIVE OF THE YEAR** for 2011 by *Report on Business* magazine.

EACH STORE PROMOTES ITSELF WITHIN THE COMMUNITY BY OFFERING DIFFERENT EVENTS, SUCH AS YOGA ON THE BEACH IN SANTA MONICA.

Many of the ideas in the **COMPANY MANIFESTO** came from founder Chip Wilson's dad, Dennis.

lululemon has designed a hood with an opening for people with ponytails. They call it the "set-my-ponytail-free window."

Chip built the company on the **laws of attraction**, using the idea that by visualizing your goals you can achieve them.

In 2010, lululemon launched a product line called **Cheer Gear.** The clothing contained a stamp that stated it was created for the "cool sporting event that takes place in British Columbia between 2009 and 2011." This helped the company take advantage of the 2010 Vancouver Winter Olympics without being in trademark violation with the Olympic association.

Y ou are a bright young entrepreneur, and you have a brilliant idea for a business. It can be any business. In order to get it started, it is essential that you have a business plan. A business plan helps you organize your thoughts and decide what course your business will take and what is required to reach your goals. Like the goal setting encouraged by lululemon athletica, a business plan gives you a concrete series of steps to follow on your path to success. This requires a pen and paper, or a computer, and your thinking cap.

Here are some details to consider when writing your plan.

1 What does your business do? Is it a service-oriented business, such as snow shovelling or dog walking, or are you selling a product, such as lemonade or clothing?

2 Determine who you are selling to. Who will buy your service or product?

3 Where will your business be located? Is there one spot that would be preferable (i.e. a busy street for a lemonade stand as opposed to a side street with no traffic)?

4 Who is your competition? How will you attract customers to you?

5 What are your start-up costs going to be? How much will it cost to keep your store running on a day-to-day basis? Is this a temporary or permanent business?

A re there other questions about your business that you need to consider? Can you see any potential problems or risks in your plan? Try discussing your plan with friends, classmates, or family members to get their perspective. Do they see anything you may have missed?

Knowledge

1 Who are lululemon's three main competitors?

2 What is the name of the company's founder?

3 What year was the company founded?

4 How was the name chosen?

5 Where was the very first lululemon athletica store located?

6 What was the name of the private equity firm that bought a minority stake in lululemon?

7 How do most people come in contact with the lululemon athletica company manifesto?

8 What are lululemon's customers called?

9 What is the name of lululemon athletica's current CEO?

10 What is the name of lululemon's signature fabric?

Answers:
1. adidas, Nike, and Under Armour
2. Dennis "Chip" Wilson
3. 1998
4. Chip Wilson made up a list of names and surveyed 100 people to see which one they liked.
5. Kitsilano, Vancouver, British Columbia
6. Advent International
7. Their merchandise is put in bags that have the manifesto printed on them.
8. Guests
9. Christine Day
10. Luon

board of directors: a group of people who oversee the direction a company is taking and have final approval over decisions regarding that direction

bottom line: the last line of a financial statement that shows the net profit or loss of a company or organization

boutique: a small business offering specialized products and services

brand: a unique name and image for a product

capital: the wealth, whether in money or property, owned or employed in business by an individual, firm, or corporation

demographic: statistical data for a group of people or population, which may include age, income and education

e-commerce: business transactions that take place on the internet

entrepreneur: a person who initiates and organizes a business

environmental footprint: a measure of human impact on Earth's ecosystems

equity: a stock or any other security representing an ownership interest

executives: people having administrative or managerial authority in an organization

grassroots: people or society at a local level

head office: the main office of an organization where most of the administrative work is done and where the board of directors meets

information technology: the development, installation, and implementation of computer systems and applications

initial public offering: the first sale of stock by a company to the public

invest: to commit money or capital in order to gain a financial return

logo: a name, symbol, or trademark designed for easy and definite recognition

manifesto: a mission statement or declaration

market: to engage in the commercial promotion, sale, or distribution of a product

merchandising: the planning and promotion of sales by presenting a product to the right market at the proper time, by carrying out organized, skillful advertising, using attractive displays, etc.

organic: a substance made of animals or plants raised or grown without chemical feed, fertilizer, pesticides, or drugs

overhead: the general, fixed cost of running a business, such as rent, lighting, and heating expenses, which cannot be charged to a specific product or part of the work operation

profits: the monetary return received on a business undertaking after all operating expenses have been met

public: capitalized in shares of stock that can be traded on the open market

recession: economic downturn or decline

restructuring: the reorganization of a company in order to attain greater efficiency and to adapt to new markets

revenue: income, or money coming in

shareholders: people who own stock in a company or corporation

start-up costs: expenses that will be incurred before a new business is able to open its doors or start production

sustainable: capable of being continued with minimal long-term effect on the environment

technical fabrics: materials that are designed for specific performance or functional properties

traffic: the number of customers patronizing a commercial establishment in a given time period

wicking: acting to move moisture by capillary action from the inside to the surface

Index